SEP 2018

D1060387

Text © 2017 by Nancy Patz and Stuart Sheer
Illustrations © 2017 by Nancy Patz
All rights reserved. No part of this book may be reproduced,
transmitted, or stored in an information retrieval system
in any form or by any means, electronic, mechanical,
photo-copying, recording or otherwise, without
written permission from the publisher.

Published by Barton Books
3526 Barton Oaks Road · Baltimore MD 21208

Distributed by Mill City Press
2301 Lucien Way #415 · Maitland, FL 32751
www.MCPBooks.com

Printed in the United States of America by
Mt. Royal Printing · Baltimore, MD
Digital scans provided by DOC
Alan Gilbert Photography · Baltimore, MD
Book design by PJ Bogert Graphic Design

The text is set in Linotype Centennial and Frutiger.
The watercolor and pencil illustrations by Nancy Patz
were rendered on Colorfix sanded pastel paper.

Library of Congress Control Number: 2017914507

Summary: The knot in Kofi's trunk is a disability that prompts
bullying by his peers and causes him feelings of sadness and
inadequacy. A story of courage, compassion, and resilience.

ISBN 9781545617960 (hc)
ISBN 9781545615317 (pb)

1. Disability—Juvenile literature.
2. Bullying—Juvenile literature.
3. Resilience—Juvenile literature.

10 9 8 7 6 5 4 3 2 1

To Maia, Sophie, Livia,
Maddy, Daniel, and Benjamin
N.P.

To Aaron Young
S.S.

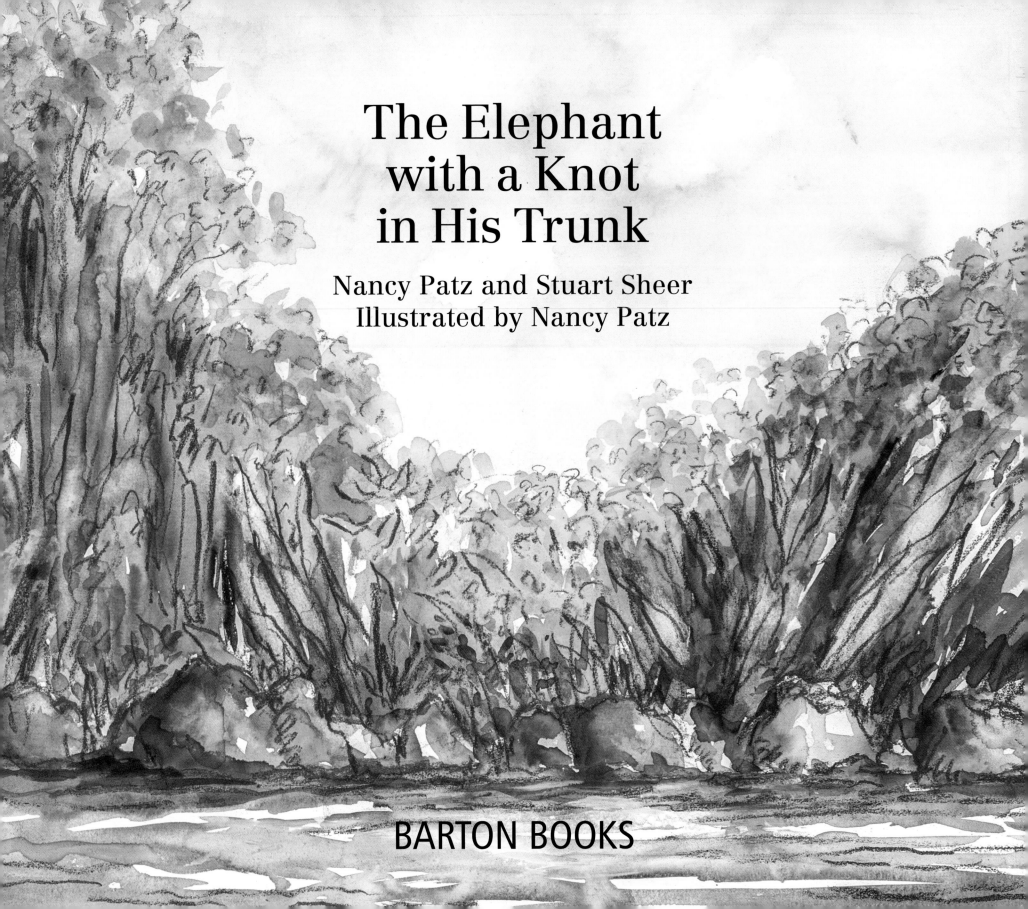

The Elephant
with a Knot
in His Trunk

Nancy Patz and Stuart Sheer
Illustrated by Nancy Patz

BARTON BOOKS

"Tell me the story about your trunk, Grandpa Kofi."
"Again?" "Again!"
"Well…"

Long ago in the greenest,
    hottest part of the jungle,
I was born with a
    knot in my trunk.

The family was sad.
"Baby Kofi has a knot in his trunk!"
"What a pity!" "What a shame!"

"You're going to be
      all right," my mama said.
She showed me how to pick
bananas and eat wild grasses
    and squirt cool mud
      on my head in the heat.

I tried. I really tried.
But I hardly could
do anything!
*I got so sad and
angry I cried.*

Sometimes I'd run away and hide.
My mama always found me.
She'd wrap her long,
strong trunk around me.

In the pond at the
bottom of the waterfall
I drank through my mouth,
the way baby elephants do.

But when I was older,
*I still had to drink
like a baby.*

"Hey, Clunky-trunk!
Go plunk your trunk! Go dunk that
hunk-of-a-clunky-trunk!"

Big Ebo, the biggest, meanest
elephant, made fun of me,
and all the other elephants
teased me, too.

When I tried to blow my trunk
like a trumpet,
the way my papa did,
I could only squeak.

"Hey, Squeaky-squeak!"

Big Ebo hollered.

SQUEAKY-SQUEAK!

The other elephants
imitated me and had
a fine time squeaking.

I wanted to disappear.

After that day I never
went to the waterfall
when the others were there.

One afternoon
when I was all alone…

SQUEAKY-SQUEAK!

a big craggy crocodile
slinked over and said,

"*Hey, Elephant!* Want me to get
that knot out? Stretch out your trunk,
and I'll pull it a little ..."

"*That's not how knots
come untied,*" I whispered.

"Of course it is!" said the crocodile.

"Just stretch out your trunk!"

I wanted so much for that knot to be gone!
So ... slowly, slowly
I stretched out my trunk, and ...

Crunch!

That crocodile's sharp pointy teeth bit deep!

He grinned his nasty smile and
clenched his teeth even tighter.

He pulled me down,
deep under the water.
I kicked and splashed as
we crashed up and down in the waves.

My mama heard us!

She dashed into the water
and pounced with all her weight
onto the back of that crocodile!

She hammered him
so hard with her trunk,
he had to let go!

"Kofi, what were you thinking?"
"He said he could pull out my knot."
"Oh, Kofi"—said my mama.

"I wanted my knot to be gone!"
"I know, Kofi," she said.

When the dry season came,
my mama, my papa, and I
set off through the jungle
to visit a special doctor.
We hoped he could
take out my knot.

I was so scared.
The doctor examined
me this way and that.

"I'll try to help you,
Kofi," he said.

He operated on my trunk.
Days later, when he
took off the bandages,
I was afraid to look.

*What if I still
had the knot?*

My trunk didn't look like
other elephants' trunks.
Mine had a curl. *But it worked!*
I could blow it like a trumpet!

Ta-rooomp! Ta-rooomp!

It didn't sound like other
elephants' trunks.
But it didn't squeak!

And now I could
teach myself…

eld date   : 3/27/2019
ickup location : Miller Branch

itle   : The elephant with a knot
in his trunk
all number   : E PAT
tem barcode   : 31267151981527
ssigned branch : Central Branch

otification   : Email Address

otes: ILL Item.
(only Howard County): (none)
aff Initials: rgv
eceive Library News By Email: No

to do the things…

elephants do!

The dry seasons came.
The rainy seasons followed.

One day, down by
the raging river…

I climbed up on the rocks to watch
as wild waves crashed around me.

The waterfall sounded like thunder,
and the river was a swirling whirlpool!

**Suddenly, out in the middle,
I saw Big Ebo!**

He can't get out!
Help! He needs help!
But nobody was there.

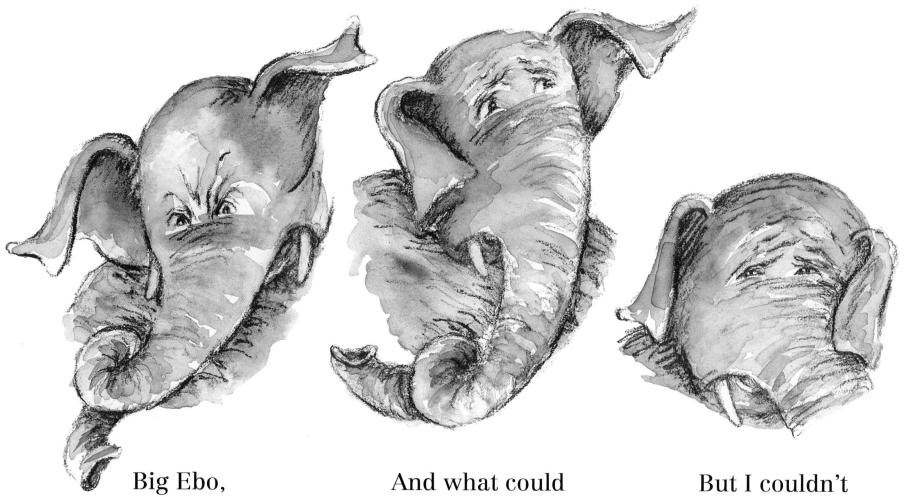

Big Ebo,
who'd teased me the most!
He'd tease me again!
I knew he would!

And what could
I do—with a trunk
like mine?

But I couldn't
just leave him
there, could I?

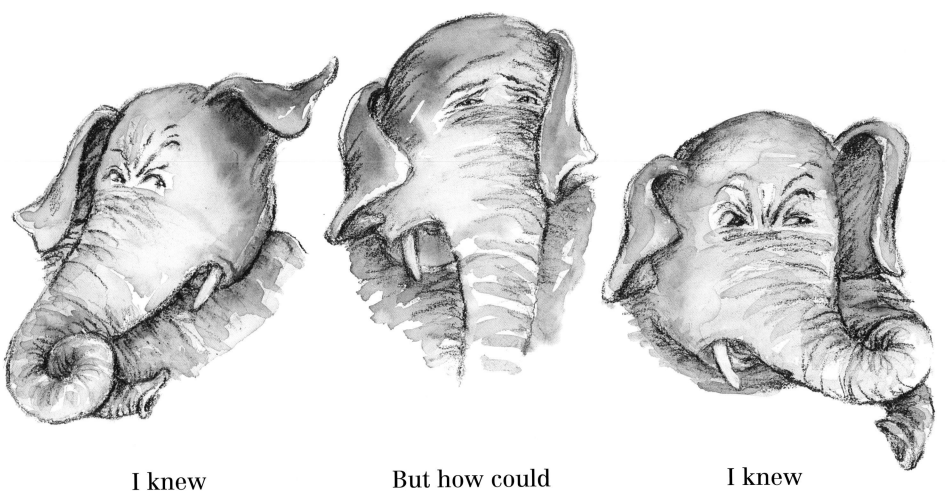

I knew
I should help him!

But how could
I reach him?

I knew
I should try!
I had to try!

Inch by inch I made myself crawl out farther on the rocks. I stretched my trunk to Big Ebo.

"Grab on!" I yelled.

Big Ebo just stared at me.

"Grab on!"

I shouted again.

Finally he reached up and...

wrapped his trunk around mine!
I braced myself on the rocks,
and I pulled. I pulled
and I pulled until ...

at last—*Big Ebo
was out of
the whirlpool!*

"You saved me, Kofi—
you saved me."

"I did, didn't I!"

I headed home on the path by the pond
where the elephants always had teased me.

And that's when I knew:
I was going to be all right!

"And I am."

"Tell me the story again,
Grandpa Kofi!"

About This Book

Nancy Patz: Dr. Stuart Sheer has a story to tell. He's seen first-hand the courage and resilience of children and adults treated for cleft lip and palate and various dento-facial problems. His volunteer work took him to Bhutan, the Philippines, Bangladesh, Cambodia, and other distant countries. Years ago he wrote a story for a book to give to his young patients. He wanted it to be about disability and bullying and the growing sense of self-confidence he saw in many of his patients after treatment.

Stuart Sheer: My friend Aaron Young introduced me to Nancy Patz. In addition to her popular picture books that make one laugh out loud, she's written and illustrated books that address such important topics as separation and loss, and how people act when they love each other. I hoped she'd be interested in my story as well.

Nancy: And I was. Stuart's photographs of his work with children in far-away villages are compelling—as is his determination to give encouragement to his young patients through a book that echoes their concerns.

Stuart: We imagined an elephant with a knot in his trunk. We were off and running. Nancy's paintings brought the story to life.

Photographs of Dr. Stuart Sheer, far left to right: At a school in a remote region of Bhutan; In Ecuador, a satisfying moment after orthodontic treatments; Lecturing and developing an orthodontic program in Bangladesh; In Bhutan, training Basic Health Unit workers to remove teeth; Cambodian boys observing extractions of decayed teeth.

Nancy Patz books, below, left to right: Pumpernickel Tickle and Mean Green Cheese; Sarah Bear and Sweet Sidney; To Annabella Pelican from Thomas Hippopotamus; Moses Supposes His Toeses Are Roses and 7 Other Silly Old Rhymes; No Thumpin,' No Bumpin,' No Rumpus Tonight!; Babies Can't Eat Kimchee! / *Written and Illustrated with Susan L. Roth;* Gina Farina and the Prince of Mintz; Nobody Knows I Have Delicate Toes; The Family Treasury of Jewish Holidays / *Written by Malka Drucker / Illustrated by Nancy Patz;* PRISM: An Interdisciplinary Journal for Holocaust Educators, Illustrations, 2014 issue; Who Was the Woman Who Wore the Hat?; 18 Stones / *Prose Poems by Susan L. Roth / Illustrated by Nancy Patz.*

For more information visit nancypatz.com.

For Parents and Teachers

When my daughters were young, my husband and I ended the day with the usual bedtime ritual, reading them books before tucking them into bed. We read many books, and many books numerous times, so much that often a child not yet able to read would turn each page at just the right time, like a page-turner for a pianist.

I predict that this will become one of those beloved books. Why? Kofi's story is compelling. As an elephant born "different," he endures other elephants' curiosity and teasing, which make him feel inadequate. At times he is so desperate he takes life-threatening measures to "fix" himself. Most cruelly, he is subjected to bullying.

There are protective factors in Kofi's life. He has parents and family who care deeply about him, who work with him to overcome the difficulties caused by his difference and seek medical attention for him. The surgical treatment helps, but the result is not perfect. He still has a flaw in his trunk. We can sense, however, that his parents' care has helped him develop a resilient coping style, perhaps their greatest gift.

As Kofi weighs the difficult decision to attempt to save one of his fiercest bullies, we see the classic conflicts: Should I try to save this bully? Am I strong enough to succeed? We can identify with Kofi's internal struggles.

We adults reading to young children will notice the full circle of life: Although Kofi has endured childhood hardships, he has successfully created his own family. We see him at the beginning and at the end of this book with his granddaughter nestled in his lap. Although the children we read to may not notice or understand the full circle, special captivating books such as this one seep into the sub-conscious. The stories we hear as children are ones we incorporate into our beings.

This book plants the concept that while bullying may seem all-consuming during childhood, one can overcome this hardship. Anything is possible if you have a strong sense of self and support from others.

I wish this book had been written 20 years ago. When I reviewed it recently, my lap felt the absence of two wet-haired, sweet-smelling, pajama-clad girls, eager for their bedtime stories. I wish I could have shared this book with them. I know they would have loved it.

Michelle Kim Leff, MD, MBA
Child/adolescent psychiatrist
Part-time faculty, Johns Hopkins School of Medicine

Who am I? What defines me? How and when do I know that I am uniquely myself? Is it the moment I look into a mirror and see only my own particularities and experience them as limitations? Or is it the moment I look into the face of another and see myself in him or her? These are the questions that underlie Kofi's story.

I believe we are most fully human, most fully ourselves, when we live in the moment of mutual self-recognition and feel the pull of our connectedness.

It is in that moment that we know, as Elie Wiesel so eloquently described it, that our lives "no longer belong to us alone, they belong to all those who need us desperately."

We are responsible one for the other. It is in the decision to act on that responsibility, to respond to the imperative to care for, defend, or rescue one another that we become most fully human, most fully who we are.

Presented with such a demand, we may reflect momentarily, as Kofi does when facing a great dilemma, on disabilities real or imagined. We may wonder whether the challenge is too great to overcome. Small, finite, and limited as we may be, however, we are up to this challenge. Like Kofi, we can choose to do the right thing.

Ann Millin
Historian, Washington, D.C.

With warm thanks to:

Susan L. Roth, Lynne Lamberg, JoAnn Fruchtman,
Nora Harrington Fletcher, Nancy Kapp, Glenn G. Berger,
Sylvan Feldman, DDS, Libby Knecht, Melissa Erb,
Tara Leigh Tappert, Sara K. Havekotte, Maida Barron,
Elsa W. Katana, Robert Berlow, Leslie Margolis, BMA
Newsletter Editors, Gail G. Green, Linda Arbaugh,
Tracy Lacis, Alvin and Shirley Sheer, David, Laurie,
Cousin Mike, Ilene, Jeannie, Peter, Susan, Alan, Cait,
Maia, Sophie, Livia, Maddy, Daniel—and, of course,
Patrick and Lisa.

With special thanks to Paula Bogert.

N.P. and S.S.

Dr. Stuart Sheer volunteered overseas
with these organizations:

Health Volunteers Overseas
Operation Smile
Dental Health International
Equadent
American Dental Volunteers for Israel